SESMA Children's Bilingual PICTURE DICTIONARY

English - Haitian Creole

Angle - Kreyòl Ayisyen

Illustrations by J. Quezada
Published by Bilingual Dictionaries, Inc.

Bilingual Dictionaries, Inc.

SESMA Children's Bilingual Picture Dictionary
English-Haitian Creole Edition
2nd Edition

Illustrations & Cover
Jose Quezada

Content & Design
Alex Sesma
Jose Quezada

Editor
C. Sesma, M.A.
Alex Sesma

Translation
C. Sesma, M.A.

Publisher
Bilingual Dictionaries, Inc.

Copyright © 2019 by Bilingual Dictionaries, Inc.
All rights reserved. No part of this book may be reproduced, transmitted, stored, or used in any form or by any means graphic, electronic, or mechanical, including but not limited to photocopying, recording, scanning, digitizing, taping, information storage, database or retrieval system, or online distribution, except as permitted under the United States Copyright Act of 1976, without the prior written permission of the publisher.

Bilingual Dictionaries, Inc.
PO Box 1154, Murrieta, CA 92564, USA
Email: support@bilingualdictionaries.com

ISBN13: 978-0-933146-11-2 **ISBN10:** 10: 0-933146-11-6

For information about the SESMA Picture Dictionary series and other bilingual educational materials visit:
www.BilingualDictionaries.com

SESMA Picture Dictionary

More than 1000 Illustrations
A simple bilingual picture dictionary with fun illustrations. Great for children ages 5-12.

Plis pase 1000 ilistrasyon
Yon diksyonè foto bileng senp ak ilistrasyon amizan. Bon pou timoun ki gen laj 5-12.

Lots of Languages
We are proud to publish the SESMA Picture Dictionary in many different languages from around the world. Find all our language editions online.

Anpil Lang
Nou fyè dèske nou pibliye Diksyonè Foto SESMA a nan plizyè lang diferan atravè mond lan. Jwenn tout edisyon lang nou yo sou entènèt la.

Hello Привет
こんにちは Ciao
Bonjour ولی
Sawubona
여보세요 Hola
你好 Hallo Olá

BilingualDictionaries.com

Buy Now
The new and improved SESMA Picture Dictionary is back! Purchase bilingual educational materials in over 50 languages.

Buy Now
Nouvo diksyonè foto SESMA amelyore a tounen! Achte materyèl edikatif bileng nan plis pase 50 lang.

Table of Contents

Chapter 0 — **Basic Words** 6
Numbers, Colors, Shapes, Calendar, Greetings, Questions, When, Where, Money

Chapter 1 — **Family** 19
Family, Age, Description, Birthday, Wedding, Emotions

Chapter 2 — **Home** 27
House, Kitchen, Bedroom, Bathroom, Living Room, Yard, Garage, Tools, Clean

Chapter 3 — **Clothes** 47
Clothes, Accessories, Style, Laundry

Chapter 4 — **Food** 59
Food, Fruit, Vegetable, Breakfast, Lunch, Dinner, Dessert, Beverage, Cook, Eat

Chapter 5 — **Health** 75
Health, Head, Body, Sick, Hurt, Healthy

Table of Contents

Chapter 6 — **School** 85
School, Classroom, Math, Science, English, Lesson, Supplies, Computer, Internet

Chapter 7 — **City** 99
City, Car, Traffic, Library, Hospital, Bank, Safety, Jobs

Chapter 8 — **Life** 111
Life, Store, Restaurant, Phone, Music, Entertainment, Park, Sports

Chapter 9 — **Nature** 125
Plants, Earth, Space, Weather, Environment

Chapter 10 — **Animals** 137
Farm, Ocean, Forest, Jungle, Birds, Pets, Insects

Glossary 147

Numbers

0 zero / zewo	1 one / en	2 two / de	3 three / twa
4 four / kat	5 five / senk	6 six / sis	7 seven / sèt
8 eight / uit	9 nine / nèf	10 ten / dis	11 eleven / onz
12 twelve / douz	13 thirteen / trèz	14 fourteen / katòz	15 fifteen / kenz
16 sixteen / sèz	17 seventeen / disèt	18 eighteen / dizuit	19 nineteen / diznèf
20 twenty / ven	30 thirty / trant	40 forty / karant	50 fifty / senkant
60 sixty / swasant	70 seventy / swasanndis	80 eighty / katreven	90 ninety / katrevendis

Nimewo yo

Numbers

100 one hundred — san
1,000 one thousand — mil
1,000,000 one million — yon milyon
1,000,000,000 one billion — yon milya

1st first — premye
2nd second — dezyèm
3rd third — twazyèm
4th fourth — katriyèm
5th fifth — senkyèm
6th sixth — sizyèm
7th seventh — setyèm
8th eighth — uityèm
9th ninth — nevyèm
10th tenth — nevyèm
11th eleventh — onzyèm
12th twelfth — douzyèm
13th thirteenth — trèzyèm
14th fourteenth — katòzyèm
15th fifteenth — kenzyèm
16th sixteenth — sèzyèm
17th seventeenth — disetyèm
18th eighteenth — dizuityèm
19th nineteenth — diznevyèm
20th twentieth — ventyèm

Nimewo yo

Colors

●	**purple** / vyolèt	●	**black** / nwa
●	**blue** / ble	○	**white** / blan
●	**green** / vèt	●	**gray** / gri
●	**yellow** / jòn	●	**brown** / mawon
●	**orange** / oranj	●	**tan** / krèm
●	**red** / wouj	●	**gold** / lò
●	**pink** / woz	●	**silver** / ajan

Koulè yo

Shapes

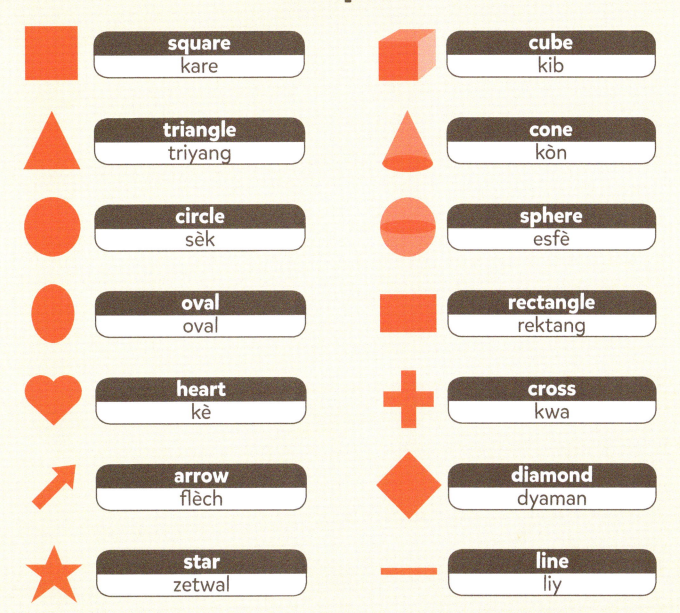

Fòm yo

Calendar

English	Kreyòl
calendar	kalendriye
date	dat
month	mwa
day	jou
year	ane
January	Janvye
February	Fevrye
March	Mas
April	Avril
May	Me
June	Jen
July	Jiyè
August	Out
September	Septanm
October	Oktòb
November	Novanm
December	Desanm

Kalandriye

Calendar

	English	Kreyòl
Sun highlighted	Sunday	Dimanch
Mon highlighted	Monday	Lendi
Tue highlighted	Tuesday	Madi
Wed highlighted	Wednesday	Mèkredi
Thr highlighted	Thursday	Mèkredi
Fri highlighted	Friday	Vandredi
Sat highlighted	Saturday	Samdi

- week — semèn
- weekday — jou lasemèn
- weekend — wikenn

- today — jodi a
- yesterday — yè
- tomorrow — demen

Kalandriye

Greetings

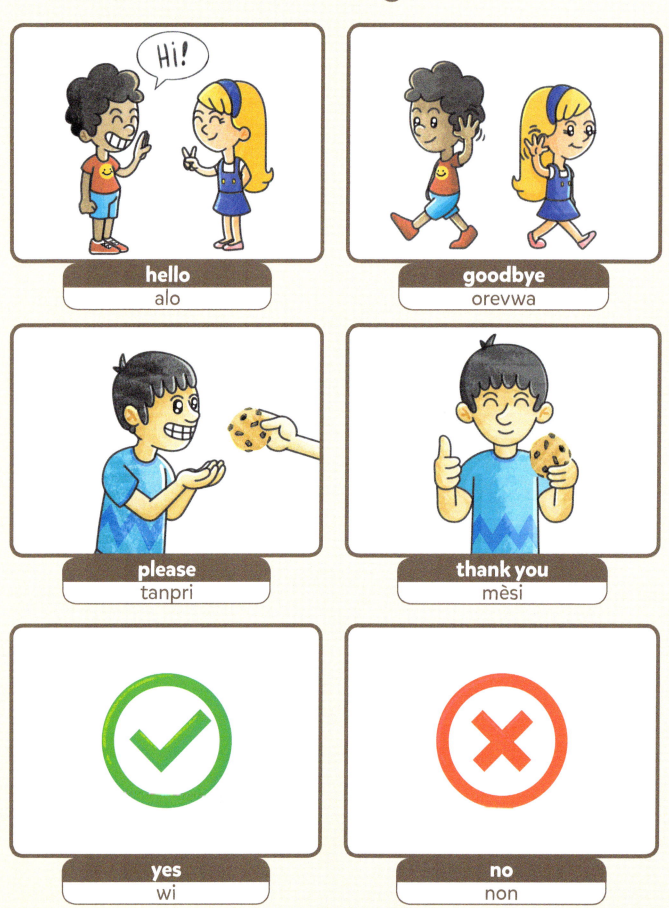

hello — alo

goodbye — orevwa

please — tanpri

thank you — mèsi

yes — wi

no — non

Salitasyon yo

When?

time
lè

twelve o' clock
midi, minui

one o' clock
inè

two o'clock
dezè

three o'clock
twazè

four o'clock
katrè

five o'clock
senkè

six o'clock
sizè

seven o'clock
setè

eight o'clock
uitè

nine o'clock
nevè

ten o'clock
dizè

eleven o'clock
onzè

Kilè?

When?

sunrise — solèy leve	**noon** — midi
sunset — solèy kouche	**midnight** — minui
one fifteen — inè kenz	**quarter past one** — inè eka
one thirty — inè trant	**half past one** — inè edmi
one forty-five — inè karant-senk	**a quarter to two** — dezè mwen ka

hour — è

minute — minit

second — segond

Kilè?

Where?

Ki kote?

Where?

Ki kote?

Money (USA)

Lajan

Chapter 1
Family

Chapit 1
Fanmi

Family

1. grandmother 	2. grandfather 	3. aunt 
4. mother 	5. father 	6. uncle 
7. brother 	8. sister 	9. cousin 

1. granmè	2. granpè	3. matant
4. manman	5. papa	6. monnonk
7. frè	8. sè	9. kouzen

Fanmi

Family

1. parents

2. children

3. husband and wife

4. son and daughter

5. niece and nephew

1. paran yo
2. timoun yo
3. mari ak madanm
4. pitit gason ak pitit fi
5. nyès ak neve

Fanmi

Family • Age

1. baby 	2. child 	3. teenager 
4. adult 	5. senior 	6. woman 
7. girl 	8. boy 	9. man 

1. bebe 2. timoun 3. adolesan
4. granmoun 5. granmoun aje 6. fanm
7. tifi 8. tigason 9. gason

Family • Description

1. handsome 	2. pretty 	3. ugly 
4. skinny 	5. tall 	6. young 
7. fat 	8. short 	9. old 

1. botip   2. bèl   3. lèd

4. mèg   5. wo   6. jèn

7. gra   8. kout   9. aje

Fanmi • Deskripsyon

Family • Birthday

1. birthday 	2. cake 	3. candle 
4. balloon 	5. gift 	6. party 
7. friend 	8. game 	9. fun 

1. anivèsè	2. gato	3. balèn
4. blad	5. kado	6. fèt
7. zanmi	8. jwèt	9. plezi

Fanmi • Anivèsè

Family • Wedding

1. wedding 	**2. bride** 	**3. groom** 
4. to cry 	**5. to dance** 	**6. to laugh** 
7. to love 	**8. to kiss** 	**9. to hug** 

1. maryaj	2. lamarye	3. lemarye
4. kriye	5. danse	6. ri
7. renmen	8. bo	9. anbrase

Fanmi • Maryaj

Family • Emotions

1. happy 	2. sad 	3. scared 
4. angry 	5. surprised 	6. excited 
7. embarrassed 	8. proud 	9. shy 

1. kontan	2. tris	3. pè
4. fache	5. sezi	6. eksite
7. wont	8. fyè	9. timid

Fanmi • Emosyon yo

Chapter 2
Home

Chapit 2
Lakay

Home

1.house 	2.apartment 	3.door 
4.window 	5.doorknob 	6.doorbell 
7.key 	8.to knock 	9.to ring 

1.kay	2.apatman	3.pòt
4.fenèt	5.manch pòt	6.sonèt
7.kle	8.frape	9.sonnen

Lakay

Home

1. stairs 	2. roof 	3. chimney 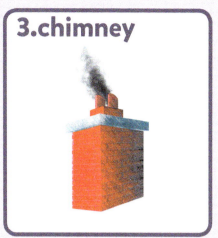
4. gate 	5. garage 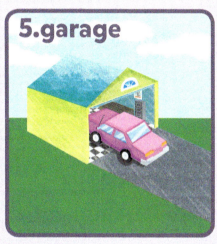	6. fence 
7. mailbox 	8. mail 	9. to receive 

1. eskalye	2. tèt kay	3. chemine
4. baryè	5. garaj	6. kloti
7. bwat postal	8. kourye	9. resevwa

Lakay

Home

1. kitchen

2. bedroom

3. bathroom

4. living room

5. yard

1. kwizin

2. chanm akouche

3. twalèt

4. salon

5. lakou

Lakay

Home

1. neighbor
2. to meet
3. to invite
4. to wave
5. to play

1. vwazen
2. rankontre
3. envite
4. salye
5. jwe

Lakay

Home • Kitchen

1. refrigerator	2. dishwasher	3. microwave

4. toaster	5. stove	6. oven

7. sink	8. counter	9. cupboard

1. frijidè   2. machin alave asyèt   3. fou mikwowond
4. tostè   5. recho   6. fou
7. evye   8. kontwa   9. gadmanje

Lakay • Kwizin

Home • Kitchen

1. plate 	2. bowl 	3. cup 
4. knife 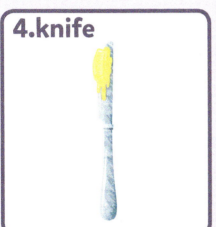	5. fork 	6. spoon 
7. table 	8. chair 	9. napkin 

1. asyèt	2. bòl	3. tas
4. kouto	5. fouchèt	6. kiyè
7. tab	8. chèz	9. napkin

Lakay • Kwizin

Home • Bedroom

1. bed 	2. pillow 	3. blanket 
4. dresser 	5. nightstand 	6. lamp 
7. closet 	8. poster 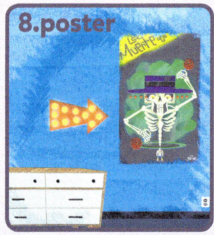	9. light 

1. kabann   2. zòrye   3. kouvreli

4. kwafez   5. tabdenwi   6. lanp

7. amwa   8. afich   9. limyè

Lakay • Chanm

Home • Bedroom

1. dream

2. nightmare

3. tired

4. awake

1. rèv

2. kochma

3. fatige

4. reveye

5. dòmi

5. to sleep

Lakay • Chanm

Home • Bathroom

1. douch	2. beynwa	3. wobinèt
4. miwa	5. twalèt	6. papye ijenik
7. panye rad sal	8. peny	9. savon

Home • Bathroom

1. toothbrush 	2. toothpaste 	3. towel 
4. floss 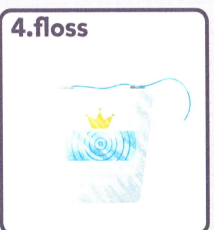	5. wet 	6. dry 
7. lotion 	8. clean 	9. dirty 

1. bwòsadan
2. patdantifris
3. sèvyèt
4. fil dantè
5. mouye
6. sèch
7. losyon
8. pwòp
9. sal

Lakay • Twalèt

Home • Bathroom

1. to open
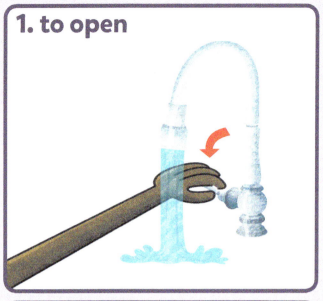

2. to close

3. to comb

4. to brush

5. to shower

1. ouvri
2. fèmen
3. penyen
4. bwose
5. pran douch

Lakay • Twalèt

Home • Living Room

 1. wall
 2. floor
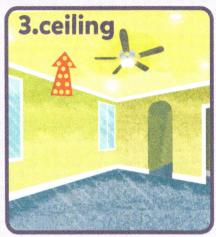 3. ceiling
 4. couch
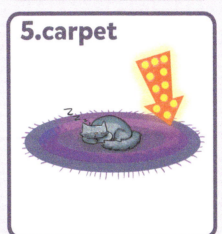 5. carpet
 6. outlet
 7. fireplace
 8. painting
 9. switch

1. mi	2. atè	3. plafon
4. sofa	5. tapi	6. plòg
7. chemine	8. tablo	9. switch limyè

Lakay • Salon

Home • Living Room

1. television 	2. tablet 	3. screen 
4. remote 	5. video game 	6. board game 
7. toy 	8. off 	9. on 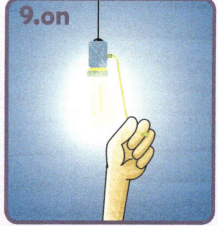

1. televizyon   2. tablèt enfòmatik   3. ekran

4. telekòmand   5. jwèt video   6. tablo jwèt

7. jwèt   8. etenn   9. limen

Home • Living Room

1. together

2. alone

3. to watch

4. to cheer

1. ansanm
2. poukont li
3. gade
4. aplodi
5. konfòtab

5. comfortable

Lakay • Salon

Home • Yard

1. lawn 	2. garden 	3. barbecue 
4. lawn mower 	5. trash 	6. hose 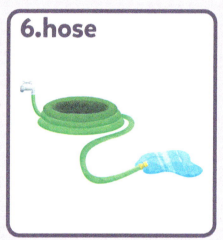
7. dog house 	8. tree house 	9. sprinkler 

1. gazon	2. jaden	3. babekyou
4. tondèz gazon	5. fatra	6. kawotchou
7. kay chen	8. kay nan pyebwa	9. awozwa

Lakay • Lakou

Home • Garage

1. paint 	2. ladder 	3. cooler 
4. fan 	5. box 	6. bag 
7. to lift 	8. to carry 	9. to fall 

1. penti	2. nechèl	3. glasyè
4. vantilatè	5. bwat	6. sache
7. leve	8. pote	9. tonbe

Lakay • Garaj

Home · Tool

1. hammer 	2. nail 	3. screwdriver 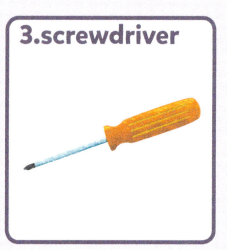
4. power drill 	5. toolbox 	6. wrench 
7. tape 	8. to break 	9. to fix 

1. mato	2. klou	3. tounavis
4. dril elektrik	5. bwat zouti	6. kle
7. tep	8. kase	9. ranje

Lakay · Zouti

Home • Clean

1. broom 	2. dustpan 	3. mop 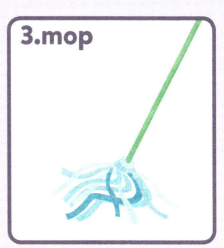
4. sponge 	5. vacuum 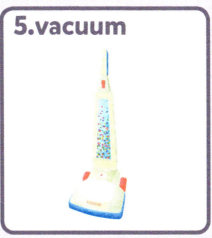	6. bucket 
7. cleaner 	8. duster 	9. paper towel 

1. bale	2. ramasèt	3. mòp
4. eponj	5. aspiratè	6. aspiratè
7. pwodui netwayaj	8. twal siye	9. plimo pou pousyè

Lakay • Pwòp

Home • Clean

1. to spray
2. to wipe
3. to sweep
4. to scrub
5. to clean

1. flite
2. siye
3. bale
4. foubi
5. netwaye

Lakay • Pwòp

Chapter 3
Clothes

Chapit 3
Rad yo

Clothes

1. shirt 	**2. pants** 	**3. shorts** 
4. underwear 	**5. sock** 	**6. shoes** 
7. sweater 	**8. jacket** 	**9. hat** 

1. chemiz	2. pantalon	3. bout pantalon
4. souvètman	5. chosèt	6. soulye
7. chanday	8. jakèt	9. chapo

Rad yo

Clothes

1. sandals 	2. boots 	3. sneakers 
4. heel 	5. sole 	6. shoelace 
7. to tie 	8. to put on 	9. to take off 

1. sandal	2. bòt	3. tenis
4. talon	5. semèl	6. lasèt
7. mare	8. mete	9. retire

Rad yo

Clothes • Girls

1. dress

2. skirt

3. bikini

4. make-up

5. purse

1. wòb
2. jip
3. jip
4. makiyaj
5. bous

Rad yo • Fi yo

Clothes • Boys

1. jeans

2. t-shirt

3. baseball cap

4. swimming trunks

1. djin
2. mayo
3. kaskèt bezbòl
4. chòtdeben
5. bous

5. wallet

Rad yo • Gason yo

Clothes • Accessories

1. belt 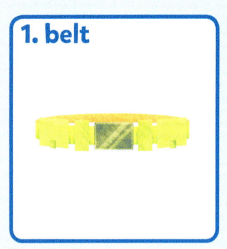	2. scarf 	3. watch 
4. ring 	5. necklace 	6. earring 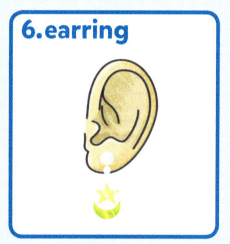
7. bracelet 	8. cowboy hat 	9. glove 

1. sentiwon	2. foula	3. mont
4. bag	5. kolye	6. zanno
7. braslè	8. chapo kòbòy	9. gan

Rad yo • Akseswa yo

Clothes - Accessories

Rad yo • Akseswa yo

Clothes • Style

1. solid 	**2. striped** 	**3. polka dot** 
4. small 	**5. medium** 	**6. torn** 
7. large 	**8. extra-large** 	**9. stained** 

1. solid	2. raye	3. apwa
4. piti	5. mwayen	6. chire
7. laj	8. ekstra laj	9. tache

Rad yo • Mòd

Clothes • Style

1. new

2. used

3. tight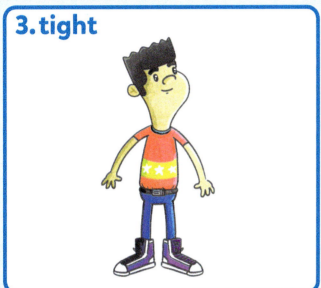

4. loose

1. nèf
2. ize
3. sere
4. lach
5. estil

5. style

Rad yo • Mòd

Clothes • Laundry

1. washer 	2. dryer 	3. detergent 
4. basket 	5. laundry 	6. hanger 
7. iron 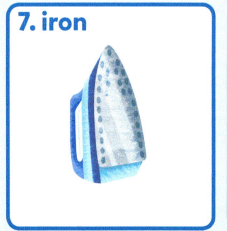	8. wrinkle 	9. crease 

1. machin aseche	2. machin alave	3. savon lave
4. panye	5. lesiv	6. sèso
7. fè arepase	8. chifonnen	9. pli

Rad yo • Lesiv

Clothes • Laundry

1. to try

2. to wear

3. to fold

4. to put
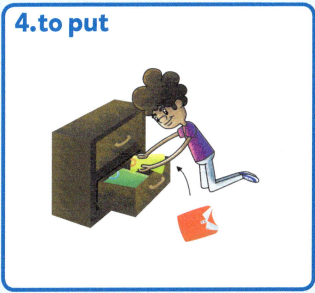

1. eseye
2. abiye
3. pliye
4. mete
5. kwoke

5. to hang

Rad yo • Lesiv

Clothes

1. uniform

2. costume

3. pajamas

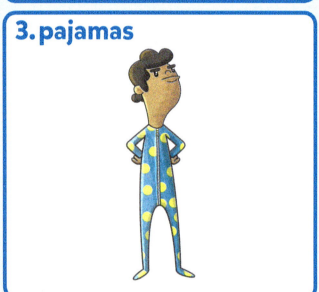

4. suit

5. robe

1. inifòm

2. degizman

3. pijama

4. kostim

5. wòb dechanm

Rad yo • Lesiv

Chapter 4
Food

Chapit 4
Manje

Food

1. fruit

2. vegetable

3. meat

4. bread

5. condiment

1. fwi

2. legim

3. vyann

4. pen

5. kondiman

Manje

Food

1. breakfast

2. lunch

3. dinner

4. beverage

5. dessert

1. dejene
2. manje midi
3. dine
4. bwason
5. desè

Manje

Food • Fruit

1. apple 	2. banana 	3. grapes 
4. pineapple 	5. strawberry 	6. watermelon 
7. pumpkin 	8. avocado 	9. blueberry 

1. pòm 2. fig 3. rezen

4. anana 5. frèz 6. melon

7. joumou 8. zaboka 9. blouberi

Manje • Fwi

Food • Fruit

1. raisin 	2. orange 	3. mango 
4. coconut 	5. lemon 	6. lime 
7. cherry 	8. juicy 	9. sour 

1. rezen	2. zoranj	3. mango
4. kokoye	5. sitwon jòn	6. sitwon
7. seriz	8. jite	9. si

Manje • Fwi

Food • Vegetable

1. lettuce 	2. celery 	3. carrot 
4. tomato 	5. onion 	6. cucumber 
7. mushroom 	8. broccoli 	9. pickle 

1. Legim Yo   2. seleri   3. kawòt
4. tomat   5. zonyon   6. konkonb
7. djondjon   8. bwokoli 9. kònichon

Manje • Legim yo

Food • Vegetable

1. asparagus

2. corn

3. potato

4. chili pepper

5. garlic

6. peas

7. rotten

8. ripe

9. fresh

1. aspèj	2. mayi	3. pòmdetè
4. piman pike	5. lay	6. pwa
7. pouri	8. mi	9. fre

Manje • Legim yo

Food • Breakfast

1. egg 	2. bacon 	3. sausage 
4. ham 	5. pancakes 	6. toast 
7. cereal 	8. butter 	9. syrup 

1. ze	2. ze	3. sosis
4. janbon	5. pennkek	6. pen griye
7. sereyal	8. bè	9. siwo

Manje • Manje Maten

Food • Lunch

1. hamburger 	2. fries 	3. hotdog 
4. chicken nugget 	5. pizza 	6. fish stick 
7. sandwich 	8. peanut butter 	9. jelly 

1. anmbègè	2. pòmdetè fri	3. atdòg
4. tchikin nògèt	5. pitza	6. baton pwason
7. sandwitch	8. manba	9. konfiti

Manje • Manje Midi

Food • Lunch

1. ketchup 	2. mustard 	3. mayonnaise 
4. salt 	5. cheese 	6. lunch box 
7. snack 	8. spicy 	9. sweet 

1. kètchòp	2. moutad	3. mayonèz
4. sèl	5. fwomaj	6. bwat alench
7. goute	8. pike	9. dous

Manje • Manje Midi

Food • Dinner

1. steak 	2. chicken 	3. pasta 
4. soup 	5. salad 	6. salad dressing 
7. beans 	8. rice 	9. sushi 

1. biftèk	2. poul	3. pasta
4. soup	5. salad	6. sòs salad
7. pwa	8. diri	9. souchi

Manje • Dine

Food • Dessert

1. candy 	2. chips 	3. cookie 
4. donut 	5. pie 	6. cupcake 
7. frosting 	8. ice cream 	9. chocolate 

1. sirèt	2. tchips	3. bonbon
4. donòt	5. tat	6. ti gato
7. glasaj	8. krèm	9. chokola

Manje • Desè

Food • Beverage

1. juice 	**2. milk** 	**3. soda** 
4. tea 	**5. coffee** 	**6. water** 
7. ice 	**8. empty** 	**9. full** 

1. ji	2. lèt	3. kola
4. te	5. kafe	6. dlo
7. glas	8. vid	9. plen

Manje • Bwason yo

Food • Cook

1. pan 	2. pot 	3. colander 
4. spatula 	5. tongs 	6. ladle 
7. to prepare 	8. to cook 	9. to wash 

1. kaswòl	2. bonm	3. paswa
4. espatil	5. pensèt	6. louch
7. prepare	8. kwit	9. lave

Manje • Fè Manje

Food • Cook

1. to grill 	**2. to peel** 	**3. to stir** 
4. to boil 	**5. to fry** 	**6. to bake** 
7. to mix 	**8. to sprinkle** 	**9. to heat** 

1. griye	2. kale	3. brase
4. bouyi	5. fri	6. kwit nan fou
7. melanje	8. simen	9. chofe

Manje • Fè Manje

Food • Eat

1. to eat 	2. to drink 	3. to chew 
4. to burp 	5. to pour 	6. to dip 
7. hungry 	8. thirsty 	9. delicious 

1. manje	2. bwè	3. bwè
4. rann gaz	5. vide	6. tranpe
7. grangou	8. swaf	9. bon gou

Chapter 5
Health

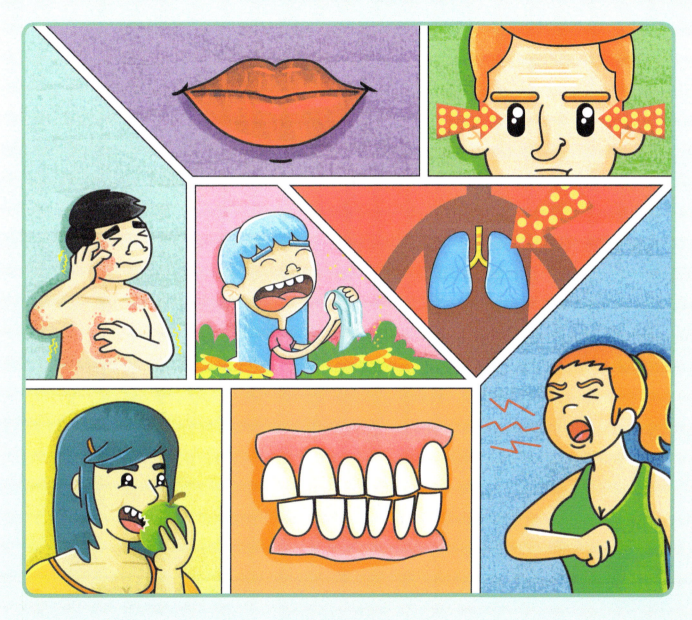

Chapit 5
Sante

Health

1. head

2. body

3. sick

4. hurt

5. healthy

1. tèt

2. kò

3. malad

4. fè mal

5. an sante

Sante

Health

1. brain 	2. lungs 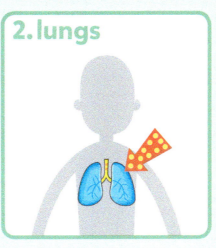	3. heart 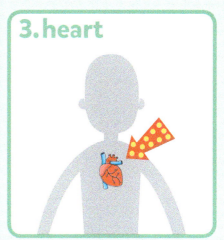
4. blood 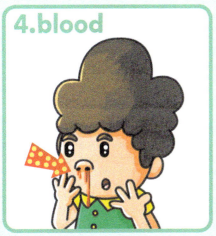	5. skin 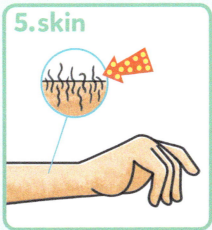	6. muscle 
7. bone 	8. skull 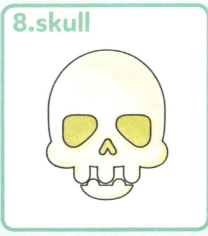	9. skeleton 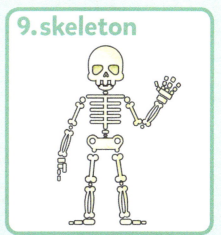

1. sèvo	2. poumon	3. kè
4. san	5. po	6. misk
7. zo	8. kràn	9. eskelèt

Sante

Health • Head

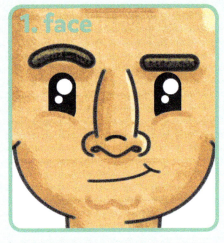
1. face

2. eye

3. nose

4. forehead

5. eyebrow

6. ear

7. cheek

8. chin

9. hair

1. figi	2. je	3. nen
4. fwon	5. sousi	6. zòrèy
7. bò figi	8. manton	9. cheve

Sante • Tèt

Health • Head

1. mouth 	2. lips 	3. teeth 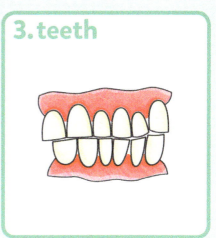
4. tongue 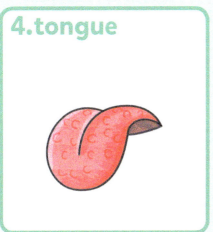	5. neck 	6. to talk 
7. to smile 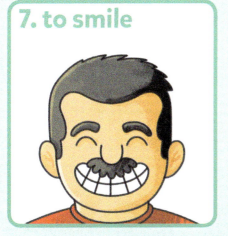	8. to bite 	9. to lick 

1. bouch	2. po bouch	3. dan
4. lang	5. kou	6. pale
7. souri	8. mòde	9. niche

Sante • Tèt

Health • Body

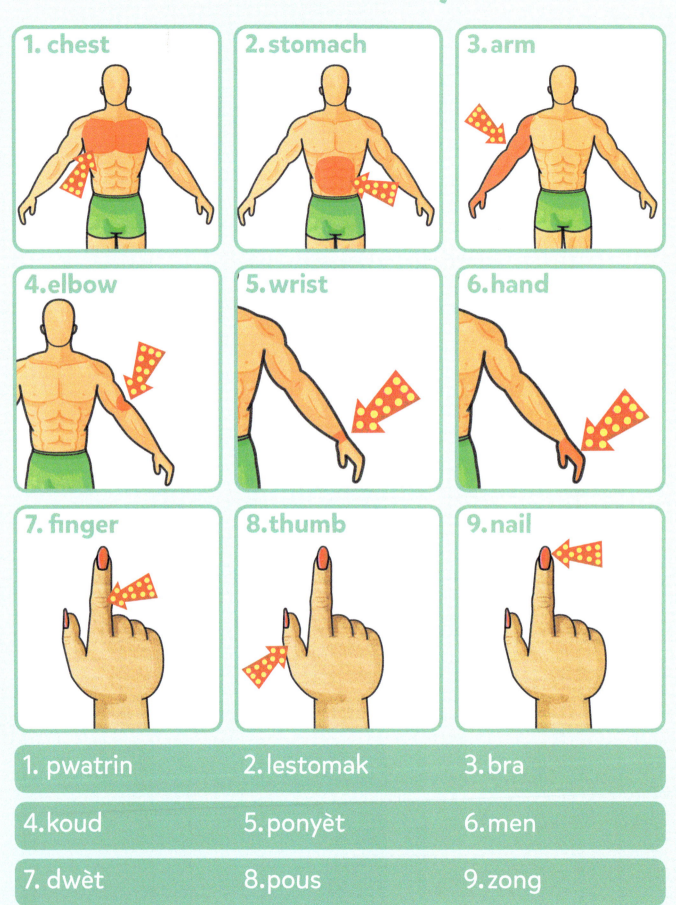

1. pwatrin	2. lestomak	3. bra
4. koud	5. ponyèt	6. men
7. dwèt	8. pous	9. zong

Sante • Kò

Health • Body

1. back 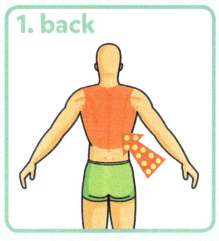	2. shoulder 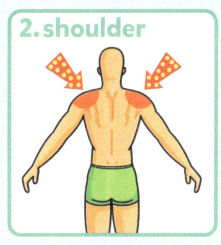	3. waist 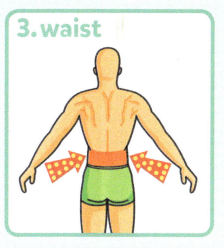
4. hips 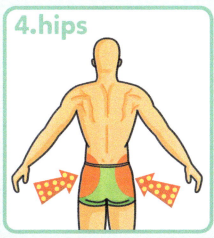	5. leg 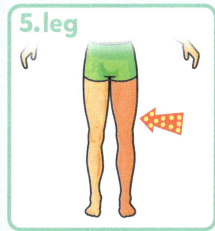	6. knee 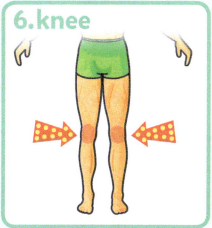
7. ankle 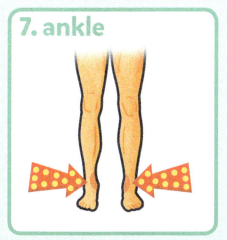	8. foot 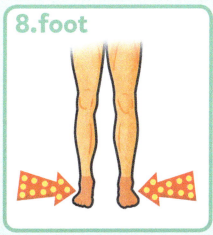	9. toe 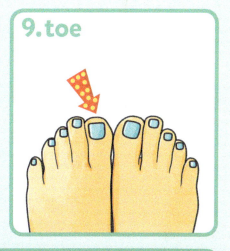

1. do	2. zepòl	3. senti
4. ren	5. janm	6. jenou
7. cheviy	8. pye	9. zòtèy

Sante • Kò

Health · Sick

1. cold	2. fever	3. flu
	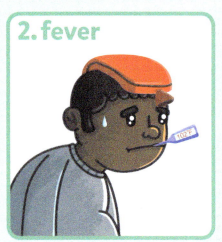	
4. headache	5. allergy	6. stomach ache
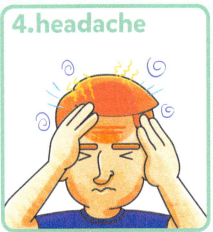		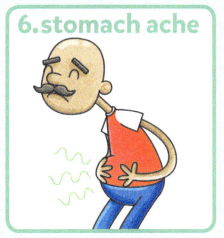
7. to cough	8. to sneeze	9. to vomit

1. frèt	2. lafyèv	3. grip
4. maltèt	5. alèji	6. vant fè mal
7. touse	8. etènye	9. vomi

Sante · Malad

Health • Hurt

1. cut 	2. bruise 	3. burn 
4. rash 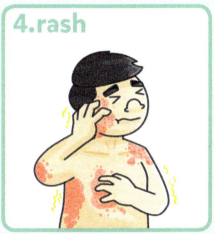	5. bite 	6. pain 
7. swollen (finger) 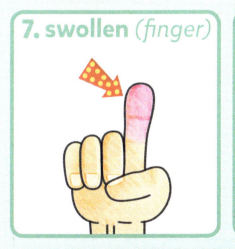	8. broken (bone) 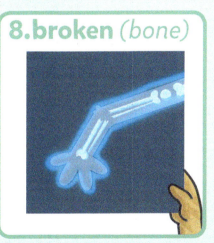	9. to bleed 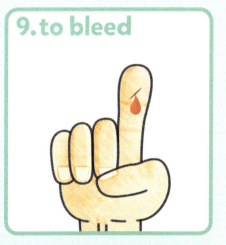

1. koupe	2. kontizyon	3. boule
4. gratèl	5. mòde	6. doulè
7. anfle	8. kase	9. senyen

Sante • Fè Mal

Health • Healthy

1. to see 	2. to hear 	3. to taste 
4. to smell 	5. to touch 	6. to breathe 
7. to sweat 	8. strong 	9. weak 

1. wè	2. tande	3. goute
4. santi	5. manyen	6. respire
7. swe	8. fò	9. fèb

Sante • An Sante

Chapter 6
School

Chapit 6
Lekòl

School

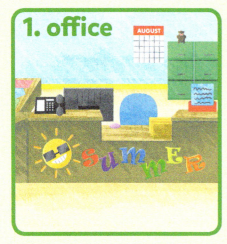 1. office
 2. classroom
 3. cafeteria
 4. field
 5. auditorium
 6. gym
 7. playground
 8. restroom
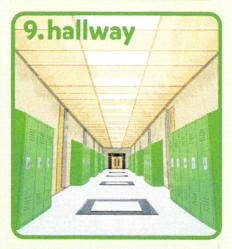 9. hallway

1. biwo	2. salklas	3. kafeterya
4. teren	5. oditoryòm	6. jimnazyòm
7. lakou rekreyasyon	8. twalèt	9. koulwa

Lekòl

School

1. principal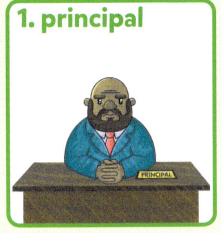

2. teacher

3. student

4. janitor

5. nurse

6. classmate

7. guard

8. fountain

9. locker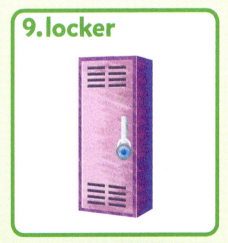

1. direktè	2. direktè	3. elèv
4. jeran	5. enfimyè	6. kamarad klas
7. gad	8. fontèn	9. kazye

Lekòl

School • Classroom

1. whiteboard	2. marker	3. desk

4. projector	5. screen	6. chair

7. clock	8. waste basket	9. flag
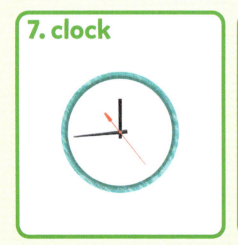		

1. tabloblan	2. makè	3. biwo
4. pwojektè	5. ekran	6. chèz
7. revèy	8. panye fatra	9. drapo

Lekòl • Salklas

School · Classroom

1. to teach

2. to learn

3. to study

4. to think

1. anseye
2. aprann
3. etidye
4. reflechi
5. gradye

5. to graduate

Lekòl · Salklas

School • Math

1. math 	2. odd 	3. even 
4. calculator 	5. to add $2+2=4$	6. to subtract 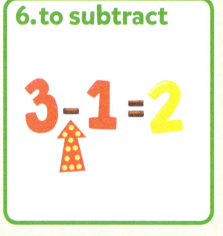 $3-1=2$
7. to multiply $5 \times 2 = 10$	8. to divide 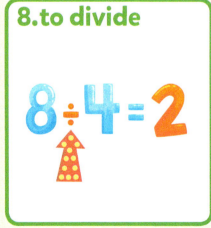 $8 \div 4 = 2$	9. to equal 

1. matematik	2. enpè	3. pè
4. kalkilatris	5. adisyone	6. soustrè
7. miltipliye	8. divize	9. egal

Lekòl • Matematik

School • Science

1. science 	2. experiment 	3. scientist 
4. microscope 	5. atom 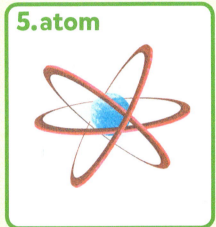	6. cell 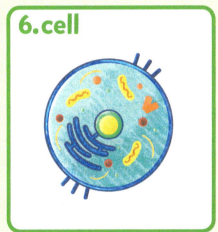
7. robot 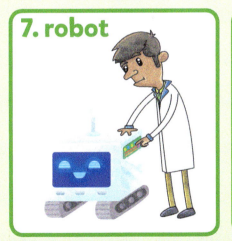	8. electricity 	9. magnet 

1. syans	2. eksperyans	3. syantis
4. mikwoskòp	5. atòm	6. selil
7. robo	8. elektrisite	9. leman

Lekòl • Syans

School • English

1. language 	2. alphabet 	3. letter 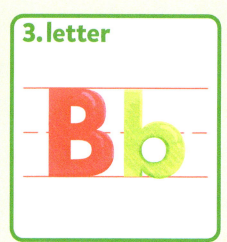
4. word 	5. sentence 	6. dictionary 
7. to listen 	8. to read 	9. to write 

1. lang   2. alfabè   3. lèt
4. mo   5. fraz   6. diksyonè
7. koute   8. li   9. ekri

School • Lesson

1. lesson 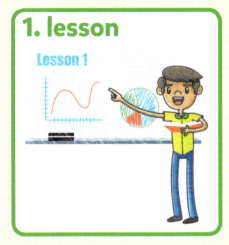	2. homework 	3. test 
4. question 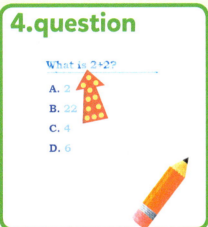	5. easy 	6. difficult 
7. answer 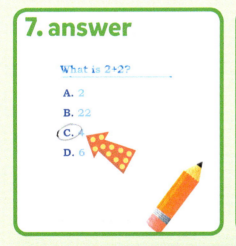	8. to remember 	9. to forget 

1. leson	2. devwa	3. tès
4. kesyon	5. fasil	6. difisil
7. repons	8. sonje	9. bliye

Lekòl • Leson

School • Supplies

1. pencil 	**2. pen** 	**3. crayon** 
4. backpack 	**5. paper** 	**6. eraser** 
7. scissors 	**8. glue** 	**9. ruler** 

1. kreyon	2. plim	3. kreyon koulè
4. sakado	5. papye	6. gòm
7. sizo	8. lakòl	9. règ

Lekòl • Founiti yo

School • Supplies

1. to color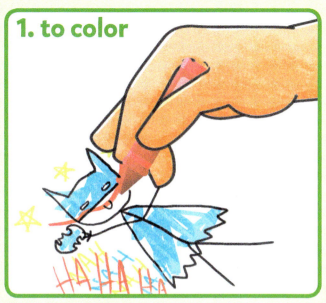

2. to glue

3. to erase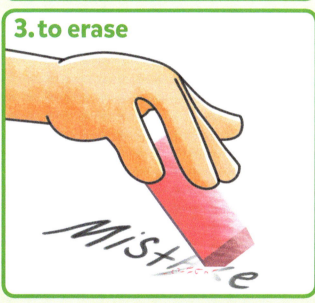

4. to cut

5. to measure

1. kolore
2. kole
3. efase
4. koupe
5. mezire

Lekòl • Founiti yo

School • Computer

1. computer 	2. laptop 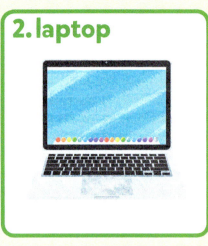	3. mouse 
4. monitor 	5. keyboard 	6. printer 
7. speaker 	8. to type 	9. to select 

1. òdinatè	2. laptòp	3. sourit
4. monitè	5. klavye	6. enprimant
7. opalè	8. tape	9. chwazi

Lekòl • Òdinatè

School • Internet

1. internet 	2. website 	3. to search 
4. username 	5. password 	6. to log in 
7. email 	8. to send 	9. to download 

1. entènèt	2. sit entènèt	3. fè rechèch
4. non itilizatè	5. modpas	6. konekte
7. imèl	8. voye	9. telechaje

Lekòl • Entènèt

School

1. elementary

2. middle school

3. high school

4. college
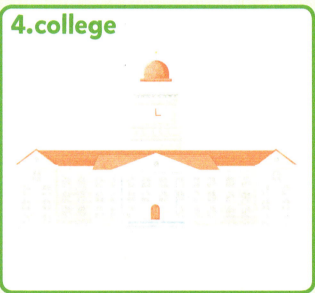

5. school bus

1. elemantè
2. premye sik segondè
3. lekòl segondè
4. inivèsite
5. bis lekòl

Lekòl

Chapter 7
City

**Chapit 7
Vil**

City

1. city 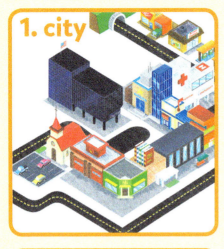	2. church 	3. post office 
4. police station 	5. fire station 	6. city hall 
7. airport 	8. hospital 	9. library 

1. vil	2. legliz	3. lapòs
4. pòs polis	5. estasyon ponpye	6. lameri
7. ayewopò	8. lopital	9. bibliyotèk

City

1. bank

2. museum

3. court house

4. auto shop

5. gas station

6. bus stop

7. parking lot

8. bridge

9. tunnel
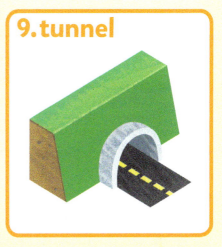

1. bank	2. mize	3. tribinal
4. garaj mekanisyen	5. ponp gazolin	6. estasyon otobis
7. pakin	8. pon	9. tinèl

Vil

City · Car

1. car 	2. truck 	3. motorcycle 
4. semi-truck 	5. garbage truck 	6. taxi 
7. bus 	8. train 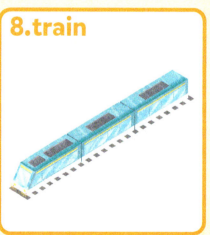	9. subway 

1. machin	2. kamyon	3. motosiklèt
4. kamyon semi-remòk	5. kamyon fatra	6. taksi
7. bis	8. tren	9. sòbwe

Vil · Machin

City • Car

1. headlight 	2. windshield 	3. bumper 
4. hood 	5. license plate 	6. tire 
7. engine 	8. steering wheel 	9. gas 

1. limyè devan	2. vit devan	3. defans
4. kapo machin	5. plak machin	6. kawotchou
7. motè	8. volan	9. gaz

Vil • Machin

City · Traffic

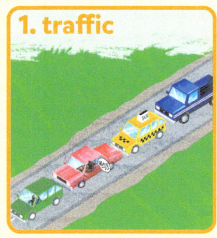
1. traffic

2. traffic light

3. sign

4. intersection

5. corner

6. sidewalk

7. crosswalk

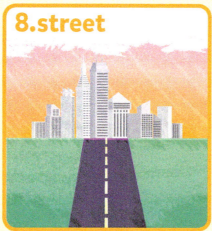
8. street

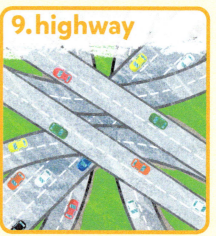
9. highway

1. trafik	2. limyè trafik	3. pano
4. entèseksyon	5. kwen	6. twotwa
7. pasaj pyeton	8. lari	9. otowout

City • Traffic

 1. to go

 2. to stop

 3. to cross

 4. to get on

 5. to get off

 6. to wait

 7. to drive

 8. to park

 9. to crash

1. ale	2. rete	3. travèse
4. monte	5. desann	6. tann
7. kondui	8. pake	9. fè aksidan

Vil • Trafik

City • Library

1. librarian 	2. book 	3. magazine 
4. newspaper 	5. map 	6. title 
7. to look 	8. to get 	9. to return 

1. bibliyotekè	2. liv	3. revi
4. jounal	5. kat jewografik	6. tit
7. gade	8. pran	9. retounen

Vil • Bibliyotèk

City • Hospital

1. doctor 	2. patient 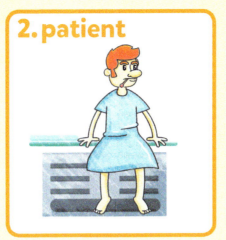	3. ambulance 
4. medicine 	5. crutch 	6. wheelchair 
7. injection 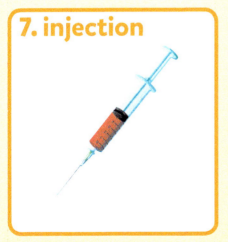	8. cast 	9. X-ray 

1. doktè	2. pasyan	3. anbilans
4. medikaman	5. beki	6. chèz woulant
7. piki	8. kas	9. radyografi

Vil • Lopital

City • Bank

1. teller 	**2. money** 	**3. coin** 
4. check 	**5. debit card** 	**6. PIN number** 
7. to deposit 	**8. to withdraw** 	**9. to save** 

1. kesye bank	2. lajan	3. pyès monnen
4. chèk	5. kat debi	6. nimewo pin
7. depoze	8. fè tiraj	9. fè ekonomi

City • Safety

1. police car 	2. crime 	3. police officer 
4. fire truck 	5. fire 	6. fire fighter 
7. airplane 	8. passenger 	9. pilot 

1. machin lapolis	2. krim	3. ofisye lapolis
4. kamyon ponpye	5. dife	6. ponpye
7. avyon	8. pasaje	9. pilòt

Vil • Sekirite

City • Jobs

1. trash collector 	**2. judge** 	**3. mayor** 
4. mail carrier 	**5. driver** 	**6. engineer** 
7. security 	**8. architect** 	**9. lawyer** 

1. ranmasè fatra	2. jij	3. majistra
4. faktè	5. chofè	6. enjenyè
7. sekirite	8. achitèk	9. avoka

Chapter 8
Life

Chapit 8
Lavi

111

Life • Good

1. good

2. quiet

3. smart

4. confident

5. to work

1. bon

2. trankil

3. entèlijan

4. konfidan

5. travay

Lavi • Bon

Life • Bad

1. bad

2. noisy

3. lazy

4. nervous

1. move
2. fè bwi
3. parese
4. nève
5. volè

5. to steal

Lavi • Move

Life • Store

1. mall 	2. store 	3. groceries 
4. cart 	5. line 	6. register 
7. expensive 	8. cheap 	9. to buy 

1. sant komèsyal	2. magazen	3. pwovizyon
4. charyo	5. liy	6. kès
7. chè	8. bon mache	9. achte

Lavi • Magazen

Life • Restaurant

1. chef 	2. waiter 	3. customer 
4. straw 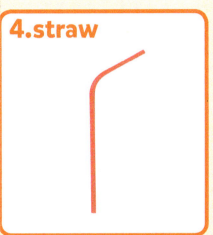	5. lid 	6. menu 
7. drive-through 	8. to order 	9. to ask 

1. chèf	2. sèvè	3. kliyan
4. chalimo	5. kouvèti	6. meni
7. gichè-chofè	8. kòmande	9. mande

Lavi • Restoran

Life • Phone

1. cell phone 	**2. to call** 	**3. message** 
4. camera 	**5. picture** 	**6. battery** 
7. to record 	**8. video** 	**9. to charge** 

1. telefòn selilè	2. rele	3. mesaj
4. kamera	5. foto	6. batri
7. anrejistre	8. videyo	9. chaje

Lavi • Telefòn

Life • Music

1. guitar 	**2. drums** 	**3. piano** 
4. violin 	**5. flute** 	**6. trumpet** 
7. band 	**8. concert** 	**9. to sing** 

1. gita	2. tanbou	3. pyano
4. vyolon	5. flit	6. twonpèt
7. djaz	8. konsè	9. chante

Lavi • Mizik

Life • Entertainment

1. movie 	2. show 	3. cartoon 
4. park 	5. bowling 	6. arcade 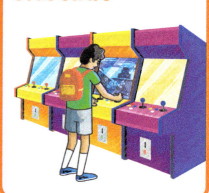
7. zoo 	8. roller coaster 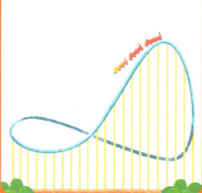	9. to ride 

1. fim	2. espektak	3. desen anime
4. pak	5. kiy	6. akad
7. jaden zowolojik	8. montay ris	9. monte

Lavi • Lwazi

Life • Park

1. swing 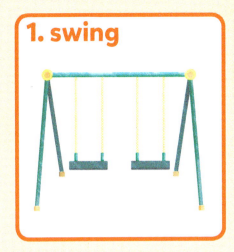	2. slide 	3. monkey bars 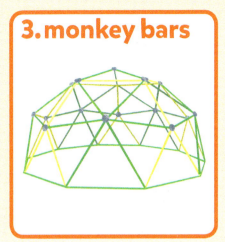
4. bench 	5. to run 	6. to climb 
7. to push 	8. to pull 	9. to like 

1. balanswa	2. glisad	3. bafiks
4. ban	5. kouri	6. grenpe
7. pouse	8. rale	9. renmen

Lavi • Pak

Life • Sports

1. baseball 	2. volleyball 	3. basketball 
4. football 	5. soccer 	6. hockey 
7. tennis 	8. golf 	9. cricket 

1. bezbòl	2. volebòl	3. baskètbòl
4. foutbòl ameriken	5. foutbòl	6. oki
7. tenis	8. gòlf	9. krikèt

Lavi • Espò

Life • Sports

 1. surfing
 2. snowboarding
 3. skating
 4. boxing
 5. wrestling
 6. gymnastics
 7. ring
 8. stadium
 9. track

1. planch	2. planch nèj	3. patinen
4. bòks	5. lit	6. jimnastik
7. teren bòks	8. estad	9. pis kous

Lavi • Espò

Life • Sports

1. uniform 	2. helmet 	3. cleats 
4. bat 	5. goal 	6. net 
7. to stretch 	8. to exercise 	9. to practice 

1. inifòm	2. kask	3. kranpon
4. baton	5. gòl	6. filè
7. detire	8. fè egzèsis	9. pratike

Lavi • Espò

Life • Sports

1. to win

2. to lose

3. to score

4. to throw

5. to catch

6. to kick

7. to jump

8. to race

9. to hit

1. genyen	2. pèdi	3. make pwen
4. lanse	5. kenbe	6. choute
7. sote	8. fè kous	9. frape

Lavi • Espò

Life • Sports

1. athlete

2. team

3. coach

4. referee

5. fan

1. atlèt
2. ekip
3. antrenè
4. abit
5. fanatik

Lavi • Espò

Chapter 9
Nature

Chapit 9
Lanati

Nature • Plants

1. tree 	2. bush 	3. plant 
4. branch 	5. leaf 	6. root 
7. trunk 	8. shade 	9. to grow 

1. pyebwa	2. touf bwa	3. plant
4. branch	5. fèy	6. rasin
7. twon	8. lonbraj	9. grandi

Lanati • Plant yo

Nature • Plants

1. cactus 	2. palm tree 	3. pine tree 
4. flower 	5. thorn 	6. stem 
7. seed 	8. soil 	9. pot 

1. kaktis	2. pye palmis	3. pye bwa pen
4. flè	5. pikan	6. tij
7. grenn plant	8. tè	9. po

Lanati • Plant yo

Nature • Earth

1. Earth

2. land

3. mountain

4. desert

5. jungle

6. forest

7. island

8. hill

9. valley

1. Latè	2. peyi	3. mòn
4. dezè	5. jeng	6. forè
7. zile	8. ti mòn	9. vale

Lanati • Latè

Nature • Earth

1. ocean 	**2. river** 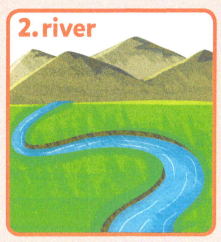	**3. lake** 
4. waterfall 	**5. beach** 	**6. wave** 
7. mud 	**8. sand** 	**9. rock** 

1. oseyan	2. rivyè	3. lak
4. kaskad	5. plaj	6. plaj
7. labou	8. sab	9. wòch

Lanati • Latè

Nature • Space

1. planet 	2. stars 	3. comet 
4. sun 	5. moon 	6. satellite 
7. astronaut 	8. alien 	9. to explore 

1. planèt	2. zetwal	3. komèt
4. solèy	5. lalin	6. satelit
7. astwonòt	8. ekstraterès	9. eksplore

Lanati • Lespas

Nature • Weather

1. jou
2. nwit
3. maten
4. prentan
5. ete
6. aprèmidi
7. otòn
8. ivè
9. aswè

Lanati • Meteyo

Nature • Weather

1. rain 	**2. lightning** 	**3. storm** 
4. sky 	**5. cloud** 	**6. snow** 
7. fog 	**8. puddle** 	**9. umbrella** 

1. lapli	2. zeklè	3. tanpèt
4. syèl	5. nyaj	6. nèj
7. bwouya	8. bwouya	9. parapli

Lanati • Meteyo

Nature • Weather

1. hot

2. warm

3. cold

4. temperature

5. to melt

6. to freeze

7. sunny

8. cloudy

9. windy

1. cho	2. tyèd	3. frèt
4. tanperati	5. fonn	6. glase
7. anpil solèy	8. anpil nyaj	9. anpil van

Lanati • Meteyo

Nature • Environment

1. tornado
2. volcano
3. tidal wave
4. hurricane
5. flood
6. avalanche
7. wildfire
8. drought
9. earthquake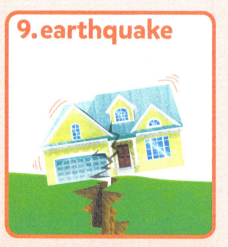

1. tònad	2. vòlkan	3. vag mare
4. siklòn	5. inondasyon	6. avalanch
7. dife sovaj	8. sechrès	9. tranblemanntè

Lanati • Anviwònman

Nature • Environment

1. to help
2. to rescue
3. to take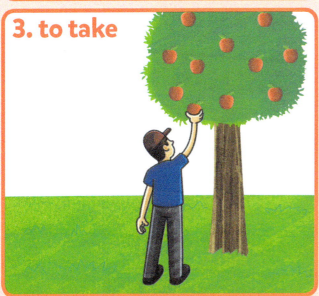
4. to give
5. to share

1. ede
2. pote sekou
3. pran
4. bay
5. pataje

Lanati • Anviwònman

Nature • Environment

1. to recycle

2. to litter

3. to use

4. to waste

5. pollution

1. resikle
2. jete fatra
3. itilize
4. gaspiye
5. polisyon

Lanati • Anviwònman

Chapter 10
Animals

Chapit 10
Bèt yo

Animals • Farm

1. cow 	2. pig 	3. chicken 
4. donkey 	5. horse 	6. turkey 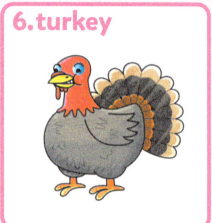
7. goat 	8. sheep 	9. farm 

1. bèf	2. kochon	3. poul
4. bourik	5. cheval	6. kòdenn
7. kabrit	8. mouton	9. fèm

Bèt yo • Fèm

Animals • Ocean

1. fish 	2. shark 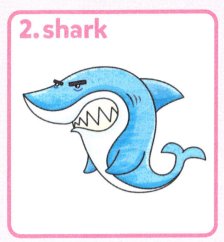	3. squid 
4. octopus 	5. crab 	6. whale 
7. dolphin 	8. seal 	9. to swim 

1. pwason	2. reken	3. kalama
4. pyèv	5. krab	6. balèn
7. dofen	8. fòk	9. naje

Bèt yo • Oseyan

Animals • Forest

1. bear 	2. raccoon 	3. porcupine 
4. deer 	5. skunk 	6. wolf 
7. fur 	8. cave 	9. to howl 

1. ous	2. raton lavè	3. pòrepik
4. sèf	5. moufèt	6. lou
7. fouri	8. kav	9. rèl

Bèt yo • Forè

Animals • Jungle

1. panda 	2. lion 	3. crocodile 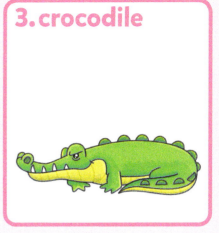
4. monkey 	5. elephant 	6. snake 
7. giraffe 	8. zebra 	9. camel 

1. panda	2. lyon	3. kwokodil
4. makak	5. elefan	6. koulèv
7. jiraf	8. zèb	9. chamo

Bèt yo • Jeng

Animals • Birds

1. bird

2. wing

3. beak

4. feather

5. claw
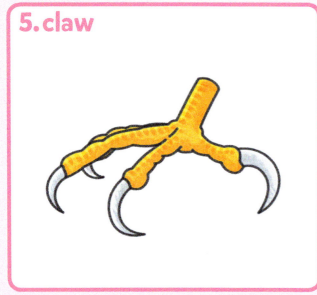

1. zwazo
2. zèl
3. bèk
4. plim
5. grif

Animals • Birds

1. eagle 	2. owl 	3. duck 
4. penguin 	5. peacock 	6. hummingbird 
7. flamingo 	8. nest 	9. to fly 

1. èg	2. chwèt	3. kanna
4. pengwen	5. pan	6. kolibri
7. flanman	8. nich	9. vole

Bèt yo • Zwazo yo

Animals • Pets

1. dog 	**2. puppy** 	**3. lizard** 
4. cat 	**5. kitten** 	**6. frog** 
7. rabbit 	**8. goldfish** 	**9. turtle** 

1. chen	2. tichen	3. leza
4. chat	5. tichat	6. krapo
7. lapen	8. pwason wouj	9. tòti

Bèt yo • Bèt Domestik yo

Animals • Pets

1. leash	2. collar	3. aquarium

4. cage	5. to feed	6. to pet

7. to chase	8. to train	9. to walk

1. lès 2. kolye 3. akwaryòm
4. kaj 5. bay manje 6. karese
7. kouri dèyè 8. antrene 9. mache

Bèt yo • Bèt Domestik yo

Animals • Insects

1. bee 	2. mosquito 	3. fly 
4. butterfly 	5. spider 	6. web 
7. ant 	8. snail 	9. shell 

1. myèl	2. moustik	3. mouch
4. papiyon	5. arenyen	6. fil arenyen
7. foumi	8. kalmason	9. koki

Bèt yo • Ensèk

Glossary

A

- above 17
- add 90
- adult 22
- afternoon 131
- age 22
- airplane 109
- airport 100
- alien 130
- allergy 82
- alone 41
- alphabet 92
- ambulance 107
- angry 26
- animals 137
- ankle 81
- answer 93
- ant 146
- apartment 28
- apple 62
- April 10
- aquarium 145
- arcade 118
- architect 110
- arm 80
- arrow 9
- ask 115
- asparagus 65
- astronaut 130
- athlete 124
- atom 91
- auditorium 86
- August 10
- aunt 20
- autoshop 101
- avalanche 134
- avocado 62
- awake 35

B

- baby 22
- back 16, 81
- backpack 94
- bacon 66
- bad 113
- bag 43
- bake 73
- balloon 24
- banana 62
- band 117
- bank 101
- barbecue 42
- baseball 120
- baseball cap 51
- basket 56
- basketball 120
- bat 122
- bathroom 30
- bathtub 36
- battery 116
- beach 129
- beak 142
- beans 69
- bear 140
- bed 34
- bedroom 30
- bee 146
- behind 17
- below 17
- belt 52
- bench 119
- between 17
- beverage 61
- bikini 50
- bird 142
- birthday 24
- bite 79, 83
- black 8
- blanket 34
- bleed 83
- blood 77
- blue 8
- blueberry 62
- board game 40
- body 76
- boil 73
- bone 77
- book 106
- boots 49
- bottom 16
- bowl 33
- bowling 118
- box 43
- boxing 121
- boy 22

Glosè

Glossary

bracelet	52
brain	77
branch	126
bread	60
break	44
breakfast	61
breathe	84
bride	25
bridge	101
broccoli	64
broken	83
broom	45
brother	20
brown	8
bruise	83
brush	38
bucket	45
buckle	53
bumper	103
burn	83
burp	74
bus	102
bus stop	101
bush	126
butter	66
butterfly	146
button	53
buy	114

C

cactus	127
cafeteria	86
cage	145
cake	24
calculator	90
calendar	10
call	116
camel	141
camera	116
candle	24
candy	70
car	102
carpet	39
carrot	64
carry	43
cart	114
cartoon	118
cast	107
cat	144
catch	123
cave	140
ceiling	39
celery	64
cell	91
cell phone	116
cereal	66
chair	33, 88
charge	116
chase	145
cheap	114
check	108
cheek	78
cheer	41
cheese	68
chef	115
cherry	63
chest	80
chew	74
chicken	69, 138
chicken nugget	67
child	22
children	21
chili pepper	65
chimney	29
chin	78
chips	70
chocolate	70
church	100
circle	9
city	100
city hall	100
classmate	87
classroom	86
claw	142
clean	37, 46
cleaner	45
cleats	122
climb	119
clock	88
close	38
closet	34
clothes	47
cloud	132
cloudy	133
coach	124
coconut	63
coffee	71
coin	108

Glossary

colander 72
cold 82, 133
collar 53, 145
college 98
color 95
colors 8
comb 36, 38
comet 130
comfortable 41
computer 96
concert 117
condiment 60
cone 9
confident 112
cook 72
cookie 70
cooler 43
corn 65
corner 104
costume 58
couch 39
cough 82
counter 32
court house 101
cousin 20
cow 138
cowboy hat 52
crab 139
crash 105
crayon 94
crease 56
cricket 120
crime 109
crocodile 141
cross 9, 105
crosswalk 104
crutch 107
cry 25
cube 9
cucumber 64
cup 33
cupboard 32
cupcake 70
customer 115
cut 83, 95
dance 25
date 10
daughter 21
day 10, 131
debit card 108

D

December 10
deer 140
delicious 74
deposit 108
description 23
desert 128
desk 88
dessert 61
detergent 56
diamond 9
dictionary 92
difficult 93
dime 18
dinner 61
dip 74
dirty 37
dishwasher 32
divide 90
doctor 107
dog 144
dog house 42
dollar 18
dolphin 139
donkey 138
donut 70
door 28
doorbell 28
doorknob 28
down 16
download 97
dream 35
dress 50
dresser 34
drink 74
drive 105
driver 110
drive-through 115
drought 134
drums 117
dry 37
dryer 56
duck 143
duster 45
dustpan 45

Glosè

Glossary

eagle	143
ear	78
earring	52
Earth	128
earthquake	134
easy	93
eat	74
egg	66
eight	6
eight o'clock	14
eighteen	6
eighteenth	7
eighth	7
eighty	6
elbow	80
electricity	91
elementary	98
elephant	141
eleven	6
eleven o'clock	14
eleventh	7
email	97
embarrassed	26
emotions	26
empty	71
engine	103
engineer	110
English	92
entertainment	118
environment	134
equal	90
erase	95
eraser	94
even	90
evening	131
excited	26
exercise	122
expensive	114
experiment	91
explore	130
extra large	54
eye	78
eyebrow	78

face	78
fall	43, 131
fan	43, 124
far	16
farm	138
fat	23
father	20
faucet	36
feather	142
February	10
feed	145
fence	29
fever	82
field	86
fifteen	6
fifteenth	7
fifth	7
fifty	6
finger	80
fire	109
fire fighter	109
fire station	100
fire truck	109
fireplace	39
first	7
fish	139
fish stick	67
five	6
five o'clock	14
fix	44
flag	88
flamingo	143
flood	134
floor	39
floss	37
flower	127
flu	82
flute	117
fly	143, 146
fog	132
fold	57
foot	81
football	120
forehead	78
forest	128
forget	93

Glossary

fork	33
forty	6
fountain	87
four	6
four o'clock	14
fourteen	6
fourteenth	7
fourth	7
freeze	133
fresh	65
Friday	11
friend	24
fries	67
frog	144
front	16
frosting	70
fruit	60
fry	73
full	71
fun	24
fur	140

G

game	24
garage	29
garbage truck	102
garden	42
garlic	65
gas	103
gas station	101
gate	29
get	106
get off	105
get on	105
gift	24
giraffe	141
girl	22
give	135
glove	52
glue	94, 95
go	105
goal	122
goat	138
gold	8
goldfish	144
golf	120
good	112
goodbye	12

graduate	89
grandfather	20
grandmother	20
grapes	62
gray	8
green	8
greetings	12
grill	73
groceries	114
groom	25
grow	126
guard	87
guitar	117
gym	86
gymnastics	121

H

hair	78
half past one	15
hallway	86
ham	66
hamburger	67
hammer	44
hamper	36
hand	80
handsome	23
hang	57
hanger	56
happy	26
hat	48
head	76
headache	82
headlight	103
health	75
healthy	76
hear	84
heart	9, 77
heat	73
heel	49
hello	12
helmet	122
help	135
high school	98
highway	104
hill	128
hips	81
hit	123
hockey	120

Glosè

Glossary

home 27
homework 93
hood 53, 103
horse 138
hose 42
hospital 100
hot 133
hotdog 67
hour 15
house 28
how 13
howl 140
hug 25
hummingbird 143
hungry 74
hurricane 134
hurt 76, 83
husband 21

I

ice 71
ice cream 70
in front 17
injection 107
insects 146
inside 17
internet 97
intersection 104
invite 31
iron 56
island 128

J

jacket 48
janitor 87
January 10
jeans 51
jelly 67
jobs 110
judge 110
juice 71
juicy 63
July 10
jump 123
June 10

jungle 128

K

ketchup 68
key 28
keyboard 96
kick 123
kiss 25
kitchen 30
kitten 144
knee 81
knife 33
knock 28

L

ladder 43
ladle 72
lake 129
lamp 34
land 128
language 92
laptop 96
large 54
laugh 25
laundry 56
lawn 42
lawn mower 42
lawyer 110
lazy 113
leaf 126
learn 89
leash 145
left 16
leg 81
lemon 63
lesson 93
letter 92
lettuce 64
librarian 106
library 100
license plate 103
lick 79
lid 115
life 111
lift 43
light 34

Glossary

lightning 132
like 119
lime 63
line 9, 114
lion 141
lips 79
listen 92
litter 136
living room 30
lizard 144
locker 87
log in 97
logo 53
look 106
loose 55
lose 123
lotion 37
love 25
lunch 61
lunch box 68
lungs 77

M

magazine 106
magnet 91
mail 29
mail carrier 110
mailbox 29
make-up 50
mall 114
man 22
mango 63
map 106
March 10
marker 88
math 90
May 10
mayonnaise 68
mayor 110
measure 95
meat 60
medicine 107
medium 54
meet 31
melt 133
menu 115
message 116
microscope 91

microwave 32
middle school 98
midnight 15
milk 71
minute 15
mirror 36
mix 73
Monday 11
money 18, 108
monitor 96
monkey 141
monkey bars 119
month 10
moon 130
mop 45
morning 131
mosquito 146
mother 20
motorcycle 102
mountain 128
mouse 96
mouth 79
movie 118
mud 129
multiply 90
muscle 77
museum 101
mushroom 64
music 117
mustard 68

N

nail 44, 80
napkin 33
nature 125
near 16
neck 79
necklace 52
neighbor 31
nephew 21
nervous 113
nest 143
net 122
new 55
newspaper 106
next to 17
nickel 18
niece 21

Glossary

night 131
nightmare 35
nightstand 34
nine 6
nine o'clock 14
nineteen 6
nineteenth 7
ninety 6
ninth 7
no 12
noisy 113
noon 15
nose 78
November 10
numbers 6
nurse 87

O

ocean 129
October 10
octopus 139
odd 90
off 40
office 86
old 23
on 40
one 6
one billion 7
one dollar and twenty-six cents 18
one fifteen 15
one forty-five 15
one hundred 7
one million 7
one o'clock 14
one thirty 15
one thousand 7
onion 64
open 38
orange 8, 63
order 115
outlet 39
outside 17
oval 9
oven 32
over 17
owl 143

P

pain 83
paint 43
painting 39
pajamas 58
palm tree 127
pan 72
pancakes 66
panda 141
pants 48
paper 94
paper towel 45
parents 21
park 105, 118
parking lot 101
party 24
passenger 109
password 97
pasta 69
patch 53
patient 107
peacock 143
peanut butter 67
peas 65
peel 73
pen 94
pencil 94
penguin 143
penny 18
pet 145
pets 144
phone 116
piano 117
pickle 64
picture 116
pie 70
pig 138
pillow 34
pilot 109
pin number 108
pine tree 127
pineapple 62
pink 8
pizza 67
planet 130
plant 126
plate 33

Glossary

play 31
playground 86
please 12
pocket 53
police car. 109
police officer. 109
police station 100
polka dot. 54
pollution 136
porcupine 140
post office. 100
poster 34
pot 72, 127
potato 65
pour 74
power drill 44
practice 122
prepare 72
pretty 23
principal 87
printer 96
projector 88
proud 26
puddle 132
pull 119
pumpkin 62
puppy 144
purple 8
purse 50
push 119
put 57
put on 49

Q

quarter 18
quarter past one 15
quarter two 15
question 93
questions 13
quiet 112

R

rabbit 144
raccoon 140
race 123
rain 132
raisin 63
rash 83
read 92
receive 29
record 116
rectangle 9
recycle 136
red 8
referee 124
refrigerator 32
register 114
remember 93
remote 40
rescue 135
restroom 86
return 106
rice 69
ride 118
right 16
ring 28, 52, 121
ripe 65
river 129
robe 58
robot 91
rock 129
roller coaster 118
roof 29
root 126
rotten 65
ruler 94
run 119

S

sad 26
safety 109
salad 69
salad dressing 69
salt 68
sand 129
sandals 49

Glossary

sandwich	67
satellite	130
Saturday	11
sausage	66
save	108
scared	26
scarf	52
school	85
school bus	98
science	91
scientist	91
scissors	94
score	123
screen	40, 88
screwdriver	44
scrub	46
seal	139
search	97
second	7, 15
security	110
see	84
seed	127
select	96
semi-truck	102
send	97
senior	22
sentence	92
September	10
seven	6
seven o'clock	14
seventeen	6
seventeenth	7
seventh	7
seventy	6
shade	126
shapes	9
share	135
shark	139
sheep	138
shell	146
shirt	48
shoelace	49
shoes	48
short	23
shorts	48
shoulder	81
show	118
shower	36, 38
shy	26
sick	76, 82
sidewalk	104
sign	104
silver	8
sing	117
sink	32
sister	20
six	6
six o'clock	14
sixteen	6
sixteenth	7
sixth	7
sixty	6
sixty-six cents	18
skating	121
skeleton	77
skin	77
skinny	23
skirt	50
skull	77
skunk	140
sky	132
sleep	35
sleeve	53
slide	119
small	54
smart	112
smell	84
smile	79
snack	68
snail	146
snake	141
sneakers	49
sneeze	82
snow	132
snowboarding	121
soap	36
soccer	120
sock	48
soda	71
soil	127
sole	49
solid	54
son	21
soup	69
sour	63
space	130
spatula	72
speaker	96
sphere	9
spicy	68

Glossary

spider 146
sponge 45
spoon 33
sports 120
spray 46
spring 131
sprinkle 73
sprinkler 42
square 9
squid 139
stadium 121
stained 54
stairs 29
star 9, 130
steak 69
steal 113
steering wheel 103
stem 127
stir 73
stomach 80
stomach ache 82
stop 105
store 114
storm 132
stove 32
straw 115
strawberry 62
street 104
stretch 122
striped 54
strong 84
student 87
study 89
style 55
subtract 90
subway 102
suit 58
summer 131
sun 130
Sunday 11
sunny 133
sunrise 15
sunset 15
supplies 94
surfing 121
surprised 26
sushi 69
sweat 84
sweater 48
sweep 46
sweet 68
swim 139
swimming trunks 51
swing 119
switch 39
swollen 83
syrup 66

T

table 33
tablet 40
take 135
take off 49
talk 79
tall 23
tan 8
tape 44
taste 84
taxi 102
tea 71
teach 89
teacher 87
team 124
teenager 22
teeth 79
television 40
teller 108
temperature 133
ten 6
ten o'clock 14
tennis 120
tenth 7
test 93
thank you 12
think 89
third 7
thirsty 74
thirteen 6
thirty-three cents 18
thorn 127
three 6
three o'clock 14
thriteenth 7
thrity 6
throw 123
thumb 80
Thursday 11
tidal wave 134

Glossary

tie	49
tight	55
time	14
tire	103
tired	35
title	106
toast	66
toaster	32
today	11
toe	81
together	41
toilet	36
toilet paper	36
tomato	64
tomorrow	11
tongs	72
tongue	79
toolbox	44
tools	44
toothbrush	37
toothpaste	37
top	16
torn	54
tornado	134
touch	84
towel	37
toy	40
track	121
traffic	104
traffic light	104
train	102, 145
trash	42
trash collector	110
tree	126
tree house	42
triangle	9
truck	102
trumpet	117
trunk	126
try	57
t-shirt	51
Tuesday	11
tunnel	101
turkey	138
turtle	144
twelfth	7
twelve	6
twelve o'clock	14
twentieth	7
twenty	6
two	6
two o'clock	14
type	96

U

ugly	23
umbrella	132
uncle	20
under	17
underwear	48
uniform	58, 122
up	16
use	136
used	55
username	97

V

vacuum	45
valley	128
vegetable	60
video	116
video game	40
violin	117
volcano	134
volleyball	120
vomit	82

W

waist	81
wait	105
waiter	115
walk	145
wall	39
wallet	51
warm	133
wash	72
washer	56
waste	136
waste basket	88
watch	41, 52
water	71
waterfall	129
watermelon	62

Glossary

wave 31, 129
weak 84
wear....................................... 57
weather...................................131
web 146
website 97
wedding 25
Wednesday.................................11
week 11
weekday 11
weekend 11
wet 37
whale.................................... 139
what 13
wheelchair.............................. 107
when 13
where..................................... 13
white 8
whiteboard............................... 88
who 13
why 13
wife 21
wildfire 134
win....................................... 123
window 28
windshield.............................. 103
windy.................................... 133
wing..................................... 142
winter 131
wipe...................................... 46
withdraw................................ 108
wolf 140
woman.................................... 22
word 92
work......................................112
wrench................................... 44
wrestling................................ 121
wrinkle................................... 56
wrist...................................... 80
write 92

X

X-ray 107

Y

yard 30
year 10
yellow 8
yes 12
yesterday 11
young 23

Z

zebra 141
zero 6
zipper.................................... 53
zoo 118